These Poems Need Homes

TO MAKE A LONG STORY LONGER

These Poems Need Homes

TO MAKE A LONG STORY LONGER

Poems and drawings by:

Dominic "Flominic" Farrenkopf

Cover Illustration by Hannah Farrenkopf
Author Photo by Wayne Wardwell

authorHOUSE®

AuthorHouse™
1663 Liberty Drive
Bloomington, IN 47403
www.authorhouse.com
Phone: 1-800-839-8640

Published by AuthorHouse   10/29/2014

ISBN: 978-1-4969-4877-9 (sc)
ISBN: 978-1-4969-4876-2 (hc)
ISBN: 978-1-4969-4878-6 (e)

Library of Congress Control Number: 2014918925

Table of Contents

Bonus Poems

Dedication

For Ma.
Who loved my poems and knew exactly...
how to make a long story longer.

For Pa.
Who continues to give each of my poems...
a kind and loving home.

Preface

Dominic Farrenkopf is an imaginative genius whose creativity is boundless. He has inexhaustible energy for not only writing poetry but for his shifting characters and points of view. His rhyming four-line stanzas gather history, coupling it to absurdity to create stories filled with joy and life-lessons. Readers will find his work enjoyable and educational as well as literary and descriptive.

"Flominic" (Farrenkopf's pen name) carries his poetic gift wherever he goes, whether it is to the public library story time, an assisted living facility tea party, or the poetry contest at the county fair. Occasionally circumspect, more often unrestrained, you will find Flominic everywhere.

Nansu Roddy
September 2014

The Story

Sitting across the table
with a great friend
listening to a tale
that just won't end.

"It was her cousin
that worked at the old store.
He's the one who found her
passed out on the floor."

"Keep in mind he'd just
moved in from out of state
and had been unpacking
that night until late."

"In that one box
he had those secret letters
written by the gal
who raised Irish Setters."

My friend paused and saw
I was starting to fade.
"Stick with me, boy,
some fresh coffee I've just made."

"I brewed this next pot
to be even stronger
'cause I'm 'bout to make...
this long story longer!"

March 9, 2013

The Intruder

It was three a.m.
kitty jumped on my head.
I pulled back the blanket
and crawled out of bed.

I stumbled through the dark
to open the door
when I saw a shadow
cross the hallway floor.

Chills climbed my spine
I broke into a cold sweat.
Did I lock the front door
or did I forget?

To drum up some courage
I reached deep inside.
I moved towards the hall
where I thought he could hide.

Slowly and stealthily
towards the hall I crept
as I approached-
into the bathroom he leapt.

I forced bravery
as I turned on the light.
I paled like a ghost
at the fearsome sight.

He was a giant
standing by the shower!
I began to tremble,
shiver and cower.

His flinty eyes
were black as polished steel.
Just before he pounced,
I let out a squeal.

My wife bounded from bed
and into the fray.
For the night intruder-
this wasn't his day.

He backed up, crouched low
and prepared to bite her.
My wife took her slipper...
and smashed that spider!

March 16, 2013

I wanted to do a St. Patrick's Day poem, so I did a little research and found the name of this town in Ireland. Everything else is fictional... or is it?

The Legend Of Letterkenny

The legend of Letterkenny
began long ago
on Ireland's north shore
where the wild shamrocks grow.

Strange things were happening
all over the quaint farmland.
Jack Campbell's prize dairy cows
had gone dry as quicksand.

Tom Flynn's brown laying hens
would only go out at night
while James O'Callaghan's sheep
bunched together with fright.

The Lower Thompson Road
was washed out in a flash flood
and Marie Kennedy's washing
was thrown in the mud.

The town gathered Sunday morn
beneath the church steeple.
They knew they were cursed
by one of the Little People.

Kyle Brennan suggested
that the town set a trap.
He'd read some folklore
on how to be rid of the chap.

They'd need seven gold pieces,
an aged barrel of scotch
and a pouch of tobacco-
it had to be top notch.

The gold and tobacco
were to be put in a sack-
a bag that held barley stalks,
potatoes and horse tack.

The book of folklore said
the bloke would empty the keg
then crawl inside and fall asleep
in the barley bag.

It was decided by all
if Pat Quinn made the nab
they'd pool their resources
and pay off his pub tab.

With six pints inside him
Quinn was brazen as a bull.
He made the snatch and ran off
with the frightening troll.

Patrick, the happy town lush
was never again seen,
but on his Saint's Day…
Letterkenny's beer all turns green!

March 23, 2013

Answering The Call

Early Monday morning
Frank's off to the shop.
His beeper sounds,
he doesn't have time to stop.

Working on the tranny
of a Land Rover,
his beeper goes off
and his boss takes over.

At Jim's clinic
it's a bright Tuesday morning.
His beeper sounds
and he's gone without warning.

His patient schedules
for later in the day.
But his beeper goes off
and he's on his way.

It's Wednesday.
Nathan has a lot of mowing.
His beeper sounds
and he's got to get going.

He comes back and says
"This job won't be too hard,"
but his beeper goes off.
"You'll have to wait, yard."

It's Friday and Joe's done
lot's of maintenance work.
His beeper sounds,
the duty- he doesn't shirk.

It's Saturday morning.
He wants to sleep in,
but his beeper goes off
and he's gone again.

There's many more
than Frank, Nathan, Jim and Joe.
Their beepers sound,
and away all these men go.

Sunday after church
they all meet at "The Cup".
Their beepers sound.
From breakfast- they all jump up.

A boy asks his dad
to give him the reason,
"They're fireman...
and it's open burn season."

March 30, 2013

The Hunt

"Did you look all the way
underneath the couch?"
"Yes, I was on all fours.
I didn't just crouch."

"Did you go through
every boot and all the shoes?"
"Yes, dad, we did.
Can you give us any clues?"

"Did you find the one
on the office bookshelf?
It was on the phone book.
I hid it myself."

"We found that one
and the two in the bathroom."
"How about in the pantry
behind the broom?"

"Yes, and the two behind
the canned tomatoes."
"Oh! What about the three
in the potatoes?"

"Yep, they were easy.
We found those three just fine."
"And in the living room?
There were about nine."

"Yes we got them all.
We found each one of those.
We even found the one
in the dirty clothes."

"And the four in the kitchen
make twenty three.
We hid two dozen.
Where could that last one be?"

"Where that Easter egg is, Dad,
we just can't tell."
"Well, let's wait a few weeks…
then find it by smell."

April 6, 2013

Coffee is an important part of my mornings. One day as I was sipping my coffee, this poetry idea came to me. I think that all people take their coffee differently as far as what goes into their mug, but they all take it the same way too. And that way is... seriously!

Morning Brew

After waking up
he strolls to the wood stack
breathing in fresh air
while sipping "strong and black".

In her robe
she sits on the patio seat
wearing her slippers
drinking "sweetener 'til sweet".

He's still yawning
as he unlocks his workshop
while gulping and sloshing
"whipped cream on the top".

Stretching on the stoop
after a pleasant dream
she stirs and sips
"mild with a little cream".

He moseys to the road
for the morning news
drinking Saturday's cup
"with a little booze".

She puts on her garden shoes
and wide sun hat
with a 'go' cup of
"a little milk in that".

A happy couple
sit on the swing and laugh
each with a cup of
"sugar and half-n-half".

There's nothing like having
your eyes opened wide
by drinking your first cup…
of coffee outside!

April 13, 2013

Off Limits

They try to hide it
in the back of the garage.
It's so beautiful-
a garden tool collage!

Rakes, shovels, wheelbarrows,
hose reels and spades,
hedge clippers, tree trimmers
and limb saws with new blades.

You move to the tools.
"Sir, you can't go back there.
The boundary is between
this ladder and that chair."

They put up a baby gate
blocking the kitchen.
To get a little better look
you're just itchin'.

Plates, cups and silverware,
a wooden cutting board,
a blender, a hand mixer
and a cookbook hoard.

You see some knives you want
and try to keep composed.
You start to sneak in.
"Sorry ma'am the kitchen's closed."

Over in the side yard
underneath a blue tarp
there's a garden tiller
and mower looking sharp.

It looks like there's a gas can
and a weed whacker,
a hydraulic wood splitter
and a log stacker.

You raise the corner
after moving a pail.
"Sir, nothing underneath
that tarp is for sale."

Tempting a yard saler most
is all the best loot-
in shut off areas know as...
Forbidden Fruit!

April 20, 2013

April Snow Showers

One April morning
we awoke to snow.
Gram looked out the window
and said, "Oh no!"

"What's wrong grandma?
We can get out the sled!"
"John, I'm worried
about my flower bed."

"My red tulips
were about to open.
That they didn't die,
is what I'm hopin'."

"My iris blades
were coming along fine.
If they got killed
I'll do nothing but whine."

"I'm quite concerned
about my peonies.
They'll die for sure
if it was a hard freeze."

"My lilac trees
were starting to bud out.
If the snow got them
I'll just scream and shout."

"Let's get the snow off
with my kitchen broom.
We might save some of them
so they can bloom."

We put on our shoes
and went out to check.
I saw some flowers
poking up their neck.

"Look at these yellow flowers!
They're not froze!"
"John, they're dandelions…
you can't kill those!"

April 27, 2013

Sweetie Pie

"Bella, will you help me
in the kitchen today?
Mommy wants to teach you
how to make pie, okay?"

"The flaky crust comes first
and it's always the same.
Choosing the filling
is the fun part of the game."

"We can make a fruit pie-
like Dutch apple or peach."
"Why only one, Mommy?
Can't we make one of each?"

"How about lemon meringue
or even key lime?"
"Mom, those sound good too!
Can we make all four this time?"

"We could make a banana
or coconut cream."
"Oooh! If we made all six
it would be like a dream!"

"We could make a cherry
or caramel pecan crunch."
"Mommy we could make all eight
then eat the whole bunch!"

"We'll make one to celebrate
Arbor Day's season."
"A pie for Arbor Day?
I don't see your reason."

"Sweetie Pie, the reason
we can make treats like these
is quite some time ago…
someone planted the trees!"

May 4, 2013

Chores

It was Saturday.
I was ready for fun.
Mom said, "No playing.
There are chores to be done."

"Go to your bedroom
and start in the closet.
Wash the clothes.
The rest- make a trash deposit."

"When you finish that,
clean underneath your bed.
There's likely more mold there
than on stale bread."

"After that we'll take
a little break for lunch.
Then you'll polish the silverware-
the whole bunch."

"You'll dust all the rooms
and then shampoo the rugs,
fumigate the basement
and attic for bugs."

"Then you can scrub
the tiles in the shower.
Then we'll take a break
for supper- one hour."

"You can change all the sheets
and pillow cases.
Then take a bath-
why are you making faces?"

"Can I go out
and tell my friend I can't play?"
"Yes, but hurry,
we've got work to do today."

"I'm helping my mom today.
I have no choice."
"Kids have no rights.
We suffer without a voice."

"Yeah, and I know well
suffering's true meaning.
It's a day with my mom…
doing spring cleaning!"

May 11, 2013

Twice The Love

It's the baby's first birthday
but daddy can't be here.
Mommy lights his candle
and brushes away a tear.

You see, daddy was called away
to heaven above.
Now mommy gives her baby
both hers and daddy's love.

She's only four years old
but she's wearing ballet shoes.
Her "dad" will never see her
and she's his loss to lose.

You see, it takes two to tango
as we all well know.
He left at the news-
mom hugs her twice before each show.

The boys are ten and twelve
and play on the soccer team.
It's game day, but dad's not there
to cheer them with a scream.

You see, mom and dad split up.
He wanted a divorce.
Now mom cheers on the boys-
twice as loud of course.

She recently turned sixteen
and so now she's driving.
As for her dad, they don't know
if he's poor or thriving.

You see, he abandoned them all
for something he felt.
Mom kisses her twice
and tells her to buckle her belt.

So no matter the rhyme
and no matter the reason,
she does the job of two
each and every season.

For her child or children
she lives for no other.
Consuming herself with love…
is the single mother.

May 18, 2013

Let It In

There's a phenomenon
that happens each year,
when the spring sunset
leaves the air nice and clear.

There's a soft wind
that will whisper at its pass,
wafting the fragrance
of the freshly cut grass.

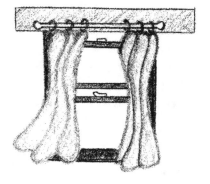

It brings the distinct scent
of the cottonwood,
growing tall since
my grandfather's childhood.

The breeze brings
apple blossom and lilac bloom,
their soft, sweet bouquet,
mother nature's perfume.

The moon beams dance
through the branches of the trees,
as they sway with rhythm
in the steady breeze.

A light drizzle tickles
the green earth at night,
causing a clean freshness
at morning's first light.

Wind chimes tinkle,
birds chirp with their voices small.
You'll never hear
a more pleasant wake-up call.

Known as "letting in
the wonderful outside"
it's sleeping at night…
with the window propped wide!

May 25, 2013

Remember Him

I remember him.
My spitting image he was.
From a toddler and lad–
to when he shaved his "fuzz".

He went from trike to bike.
A car was his next plan.
Drafted when he bought it–
my son became a man.

I remember him.
My little bundle of joy.
He clung to my side–
he was mama's little boy.

He grew tall and strong,
was head and shoulders above.
Before he shipped out
he married his second love.

I remember him.
I would often tag along.
He would always have a joke–
or a silly song.

I was his maid of honor
and little sister.
I cried knowing he'd leave
soon after he kissed her.

I remember him.
He held the door and my chair,
complimented my dresses
and my curly hair.

He was a true gentleman.
I, his blushing bride.
His leaving left me mixed
with bitterness and pride.

I remember him
in photo albums alone.
I viewed his short life
in the pictures I was shown.

Mother told me
he fell at the enemy's gun.
He never came home
to hold me, his only son.

"I remember him
by passing him on to you.
Your dear grandfather died
for the Red, White and Blue."

My daughter climbed my lap,
a tear started to brim.
"Show me too Daddy...
so I can remember him."

June 1, 2013

The Apron

On the first day of kindergarten
your eyes had tears.
I dried them with my apron
then hugged away your fears.

What you didn't know
is that when you walked out the door,
I bawled into that apron
for an hour or more.

In first grade you traced your hand
into a little patch,
I sewed it to the apron
where I had snagged a latch.

In second grade for your class
I baked your birthday cake.
In third grade I wore it
to make your lunch for the lake.

We made you a volcano
for fourth grade science fair.
Fifth grade scout meetings
as den mother, it's what I'd wear.

Sixth, seventh and eighth
there was always a bake sale.
Making baked treats
I wore the apron without fail.

The next year as a freshman
you started high school,
I showed up at class with it on.
That was not cool.

Tenth and eleventh
the garage was your special place,
with my apron I'd dab at
the grease spots on your face.

All through this senior year
in it I would wring my hands,
as you confidently formulated
life's big plans.

Today as you fling your cap
and spread your brand new wings,
I'll dry my eyes once more…
as I cut the apron strings!

June 8, 2013

School's Out

Back in September
I had to take an assigned seat
and into my head
facts and figures the teacher beat.

"A train leaves from Chicago
traveling to the west-
pay close attention
this will be on the next math test."

"When Lincoln was president
what queen was on the throne?
You'll need this information
when you're out on your own."

"Don't end a sentence
with a preposition of course.
You'll find this quite useful
when you enter the workforce."

"Recite the components
of a zinc molecule.
Without this knowledge
you could face much ridicule."

"Describe in depth
the endoplasmic reticulum.
It's a vital part
of your science curriculum."

We were studying
Jupiter's fifty seventh moon
when we were saved by
the precious, cherished month of June.

For the last nine months
we studied, were lectured and quizzed.
We poured over our text books
until our brains were frizzed.

Now that it's summer
I'm not gonna study at all.
In fact I've only got three months…
to forget it all!

June 15, 2013

Conner Bridge

We took a drive last night
down to Conner bridge.
The evening sun rested
on Trapper's south ridge.

Audrey pulled the car
over to the shoulder.
"Though sixty years passed,
the river's no older."

We scrambled down
the steep bank to the river.
I looked around
and couldn't help but shiver.

The giant cottonwoods
still loomed overhead.
Their pitch pods covered the rocks
a dark brown-red.

The Bitterroot River
still played the same tune
we heard in our youth
in the middle of June.

"I'll race you Judy Lu,
to dad's fishing hole!"
We dashed off downstream,
I gave her dress a pull.

"That's cheating, sis!
I'll tell daddy, I will.
Just as soon as he gets home
from the sawmill."

"Oh, don't tattle Audrey,
then the fun won't last!
Don't tell on me
and I'll let you have first cast."

"We rounded the bend
and there, to our surprise,
was Dad with a fishing pole.
"Hey there, you guys!"

"Okay Audrey, you're up first
cast it out far.
Judy help yourself
to sweet tea in that jar."

"Tell us how your day went.
Was it hot and long?"
"Oh girls, I'd rather teach you
this funny song!"

"Judy, are you all right?"
Audrey shook my arm.
"Just reminiscing.
Didn't mean any harm."

"Let's get going, but first-
tuck the fish in bed."
"Oh, that's the silly phrase
Daddy always said!"

"Daddy would tell us that-
we'd giggle and squirm.
Oh what fun we had with him…
drowning a worm!"

June 22, 2013

Summer's First

The Monday morning
after a nice weekend
the office staff meets
and everyone's a friend.

"I took the boat out
and fried both of my thighs.
We caught lots of fish-
all of them a good size."

"I went to the lake
and baked both my shoulders.
We swam all afternoon
and dove from boulders."

"I hiked to the falls
and got a crispy neck.
After the long hike
I was a frazzled wreck."

"I put in my garden
I must have a knack-
I broiled myself
in the small of my back."

"I went for a spin
past the fields and farms.
It was a great bike ride
but I cooked my arms."

"I had a softball tourney
I played first base.
We took third overall
but I seared my face."

I love these meetings
so I can quickly learn
how everyone achieved…
summer's first sunburn!

June 29, 2013

I've heard of fisherman using unconventional methods to catch fish. I bet this would work.

The Fly

I'd been fishing the river
since morning's first light.
And despite my efforts
I hadn't had a bite.

I started casting
while the morning fog was thick.
I thought a sinking fly line
would be just the trick.

A salmonfly nymph
was the first off of my vest.
I tried it for a while
giving it my best.

I waded downstream
and tried a salmonfly dry.
The mist had cleared up
revealing a clear blue sky.

I used golden stone nymphs
into mid-afternoon-
then switched to golden stone drys.
Same song- different tune.

I started stalking
towards a really deep pool.
T'was early evening.
I'd be no fishes' fool.

I unzipped my fly vest
and reached beneath my shirt.
I tied a special fly
and then cast with a spurt.

I used a roll cast
and landed right in a run.
I dead drifted my new fly
and son of a gun!

A massive trout rose
and for the first time in print
a catch is confirmed...
using belly button lint!

July 6, 2013

As children, we used to have so much fun in the summer with fireworks.
This poem was a cinch to write... drawing from all of my experience!

Fireworks

Each July I go
to the fireworks stand
and I load up with
pyrotechnics in hand!

I exploded
a Green Dragon Sparking Tweet
right at prissy Patty's
perfect little feet!

A red Back-Flash Race Car
I lit with a torch
and raced it across
old man Williams' front porch!

I left my sister, Maggie,
with shaky knees
after launching at her
Lightning Strike Black Bees!

I scared the be-jeebers
out of the milkman
with fifty Bam-Bam Blasters
in the trash can!

I booby-trapped
the front lawn of Mrs. Rhodes
with Captain Colossal
Lethal Landmine Loads!

I surprised some boys
on their skatey-scooters
by barraging them
with Zinging Star Shooters!

In the garden I lit
a Gorilla Bomb
and I discovered a short fuse…
on my mom!

July 13, 2013

She Once Was

It's her wedding day.
She lowers her white veil,
turns gracefully
and down the aisle sets sail.

She once was an infant
just learning how to walk
and cutely forming new words
as she learned to talk.

Soon it was tea parties,
dolls and a bike to ride,
a playhouse, wading pool
and a slip-n-slide.

Up-all-night sleepovers
and talking on the phone
trying out make-up
and wanting to be alone.

Shoes, accessories
and clothes with a high price tag,
tanning, hair, nails
and a designer handbag.

Letterman jackets, yearbooks
and the senior prom,
graduation gowns, tassels,
a cheerleading pom.

Next came college life
and studying late at night
earning her degree
she also found "Mr. Right".

She had come so far
to reach her magical day
her bright future resembled
a new block of clay.

Walking up the aisle
and just bursting with pride
replaying her youth…
was the father of the bride!

July 20, 2013

The tip used in this poem is proven effective. Most people I talked to when researching this poem confirmed using this method successfully.

Hot Bed

Bearing the heat
of a hot summer day
is carried along
when night comes its way.

To beat the heat
I have devised a plan.
The first thing you'll need
is a high-speed fan!

Set the fan up
to blow across the bed.
Move around that air
that's stagnant and dead!

Right before bed
prop the window open.
For a cool breeze
is what you're hopin'!

Now for pajamas.
Make sure they are thin
and of a fabric
that won't stick to skin.

Get a cold drink
set it on your night stand.
You want to keep that baby
close at hand!

Next is a trick
I learned from a geezer.
Keep your top sheet-
all day in the freezer!

Toss that sheet on
and hop into the sack!
Sprawl out spread-eagled
lying on your back!

The final trick-
that works without a doubt.
If you're still too hot…
just kick one leg out!

July 27, 2013

Off The Vine

After a full day
in the irrigation ditch
pluck it out, slice it
and eat like the royal rich!

Cut it in long spears
half moon slices or wedges
then spit the seeds
over the bushes and hedges!

You can have a contest
for distance and best aim.
Eating the most, fastest
is also a fun game!

Then you play the game
"Chuck the rind at my sister".
With juice on her shirt
you can't tell mom you missed her!

Dad chops off the end
and then eats it like a bowl.
Grandpa pours on some salt
which I find rather dull!

I've never tried this-
not sure if it's fun or dumb
cut out a cork
and pour in a bottle of rum!

Buy from the roadside stand
what the farm can yield
or wait for dark
and pinch one out of the field!

Many a straight has risked
becoming a felon-
snitching this summertime fruit...
the watermelon!

August 3, 2013

I think every family has people like these. If not... they're missing out!

The Reunion

Uncle Joe tears up
in a beat up pickup truck.
He never washes it
'cause that would be bad luck.

His clothes are tattered
and he's got moonshine in jugs.
Here comes Uncle Ed
who gives rear-out awkward hugs.

Grandma Lynn's now slimmer
and Grandpa Tom's 'bout deaf
but during the football game
he still likes to ref.

My sister Claire now smokes
at least two packs a day.
Her boyfriend Grant
wants money he'll never repay.

Wearing hemp clothing
is my organic "Aunt Bean".
She rode her bike 200 miles-
she's that "green".

My cousin Gina
has a husband with money.
She struts around with wine
calling us all "Honey".

Cousins twice removed
are Bonnie and Monica.
Talent night with their nose-
they play harmonica.

Old Grandpa Dave
and even older Uncle Nate
talk about their wills
and which of us just can't wait.

Cousin Isaac's not here.
He got a "promotion".
But we know he's on a cruise
out on the ocean.

My wife's stuck in the kitchen
cooking all the food
and straightening the kids out
who are being rude.

Not unlike a circus sideshow
you'd pay to see-
we've got great characters…
I call my family!

August 10, 2013

Cloudburst

"Another dry one"
the weather man's saying
the farmers shake their heads
and they start praying.

At the Forest Service
danger is higher.
The rangers worry
about forest fire.

Several ditches' head gates
will now have to close.
Gardeners watch dust blow
from their drying rows.

River water temps rise
while the levels drop.
Early afternoon
the fishing has to stop.

Throughout the neighborhood
lawns are turning brown.
There's watering restrictions
all across town.

The mountain's creeks
now flow as a weak trickle.
Their trout populations
are in a pickle.

The weeks drag on by
without a drop of rain-
suddenly there's droplets
on the window pane!

We raced to the door
and saw that we're not cursed.
I exclaimed over
the powerful cloudburst:

"For this rain
we've all been prayin' and hopin'.
Hey Joe. Did you know…
your car window's open?"

August 17, 2013

Oftentimes people will assume that I am the main character in the poems I write, not realizing they are purely fictional. I usually just dismiss the comments I receive with a small chuckle. Well, when I wrote this poem I didn't laugh for long. The outpouring of comments from readers who thought that this was my way of announcing a pregnancy was overwhelming! Needless to say, my wife was bombarded with comments, questions and congratulations. I was bombarded from her with: "Why did you write that!?" Thankfully my wife has a sense of humor and the repercussions of this poem have *almost* blown over.

Cravings

"Sweetie Pie, I'm hungry.
Can you pop out of bed,
run down to the store
and buy me potato bread?"

"Also get spicy mustard
and some honey ham,
dark chocolate fudgesicles
and boysenberry jam."

"I know we just had supper,
but Dear could you please,
go to the store and get me
Monterey Jack cheese?"

"Buy peaches, fish sticks,
root beer and a pretzel twist.
Keep your phone handy-
I might text you a new list."

"Sugar, I know you just
put your pajamas on,
but can you go see
if the doughnuts are all gone?"

"Buy me a maple bar
and one filled with sweet cream.
Get bread and butter pickles too-
they make me dream."

"Love, it's almost dawn
and I'm hungry for fruit cake,
maple syrup, bread sticks
and a strawberry shake."

All hours of the night
I'm out food collecting.
It's all weird stuff too because…
my wife's expecting!

August 24, 2013

The Ice Cream Truck

"All around the mulberry bush…"
the bell dings.
Announcing great delights
the ice cream truck brings.

All summer long
I've been enjoying these treats-
hours and hours
of indulging on sweets.

I squeeze from my tire swing,
run to the south
and throw away the lolli
that's in my mouth.

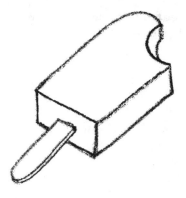

I think I'll order
a creamy orange dream bar.
The truck's two blocks over-
that's really not far.

I'll also get a turtle crunch-
they're the best.
After half of a block
I needed a rest.

To catch my breath
I leaned against an oak tree
and dreamed of rocky road-
all marshmallowy!

As the tinkling bell
continued on its way
I thought, "I'll buy
a tropical twist today."

I resumed jogging
hoping for a milkshake
and a huge slice
of coconut ice cream cake.

The ice cream truck
sounded further away now.
I was huffing and puffing
like an old cow.

My dreams of a
banana-strawberry freeze
drifted slowly away
on the summer breeze.

I'm way up in my weight
and down on my luck.
I've had too much ice cream…
so I've missed the truck!

August 31, 2013

Dear Diary

Dear Diary, though late,
I just have to say
I had the most wonderful,
fantastic day!

I walked to town
and went to the county fair.
I strolled around
hoping to see some friends there.

I ordered some ice cream
when he caught my eye.
Tall and slender, with blonde hair–
a handsome guy!

He caught me looking
and flashed a bright smile.
Then bold as brass
he came to sit awhile.

Like a real gentleman,
he asked my name.
Blushing, I smoothed my dress
and asked him the same.

To the carnival,
he asked to escort me.
My heart fluttered
like wings of a dove set free.

He showed off with the hammer
and rang the bell.
Won me a prize-
threw more balls than I can tell.

The carnival lights
danced in his dreamy eyes.
My true feelings for him
I could not disguise.

It felt so natural
when he took my hand
and led the way
to the cotton candy stand.

We bought a bag
of fluffy pink and teal
then bought two tickets
for the Ferris wheel.

We stood in line talking
as the night wore on.
We got in the seat
and then the crowd was gone.

His lips touched mine-
'twas carnival night true bliss-
tasting of cotton candy…
was my first kiss!

September 7, 2013

A Good Morning

This morning my husband
barely made it out of bed.
Let's just say he's not as spry as
when first we were wed!

He pulled the down comforter back
like it weighed a ton
shuffled towards the bathroom-
the closest thing to a run!

He made it to the bathroom
and then- oh my the noise!
The embarrassing sounds
that amuse all little boys!

He has to have his bathrobe
'cause he's always colder.
He barely wrestled it on
'cause of his bad shoulder!

He shuffled down the hall
but then he had to go back.
He forgot his glasses.
Without them he can't see "jack"!

He came down the stairs
with lots of creaking and squeaking.
It's his knees and ankles
and his back that needs tweaking!

He shuffled to the cupboard,
took a handful of pills-
too numerous to tell-
they comfort his aches and ills!

He sat at the table
in front of prune juice and toast,
picked up the paper
and turned to the part he likes most!

"Darling why are you smiling?
Aren't you feeling your age?"
"Jean, it's 'cause I'm not on…
the obituary page!"

September 14, 2013

Under The Lights

Monday afternoon
it's warm-up drills,
drop back passing lines
and blocking skills.

We work on endurance
with line sprints,
play "king of the hill"
with no coach hints.

Tuesday we focus on
direct snaps,
double teaming
and blowing the gaps.

We practice
skeleton backfield-
then play "gauntlet"
or "no man yield".

Wednesday brings
alley drill and stalk block,
hurry-up offense
to beat the clock.

We use the no huddle
and trick plays,
do hand off lines
and then "loose ball craze".

Half contact scrimmage
is played Thursday.
Remind the defense
to hit that way.

Zone coverage drills
and interceptions,
"on my count"
and play call corrections.

At pep rally
we make lots of noise.
Coach calls us in
and steadies us boys.

The captain calls,
"On three- go team, fight!"
We storm the field...
it's Friday night!

September 21, 2013

Out Back

If us boys got caught
smoking in the school's,
we'd have to whitewash it
and look like fools.

The one at the church
had a latch that would stick.
Preacher got stuck once.
He broke out with a kick.

Big Rick's Saloon's
was always in disrepair.
As you probably guessed
it got lots of wear.

We'd lock our sisters in
and they'd always snitch.
So we'd end up behind there
gettin' the switch.

Each Halloween we'd knock
Old Man Edward's down.
He'd chase after us
in his flannel night gown.

Boiling hot in summer-
ice cold in winter.
Careful of the old ones-
you'd get a splinter.

The bank president's
had ornate scroll woodwork.
The mayor's had a skylight
for a nice perk.

Most people's were plain
with just one coat of paint.
Ours was no exception-
small and rather quaint.

It had no running water
for hands to douse.
A plain two-seater...
was our family's outhouse!

September 28, 2013

The Magazine

I was at the doctor's office
in the waiting room
when I picked up the June issue
of Women Can Bloom.

The cover story was about
a young girl named Kate
whose grades and skin improved
when she lost a lot of weight.

There was a flowery poem
about a girl in France
who lost enough weight
that she could finally slow dance.

There was a romance story
of a woman and man
who met at a weight loss clinic
and away they ran.

The featured celebrity
was a fast rising star
who rose above photos
of her and her cookie jar.

I just skimmed the section called
"Diet of the Month Club".
I knew the cake recipe
was Chocolate Butter-Tub.

I turned the page
for a very unpleasant surprise.
It seemed the magazine
was not helping someone's size.

"Ma'am, you're next. Go ahead
and bring that magazine back."
"Nope. The cake recipe's gone…
I'll leave it on the stack."

October 5, 2013

A Crisp Morning

I stepped out this morning
and breathed in crisp, fall air.
I saw we had white icing
almost everywhere.

The lawn was still green
but it was all long sharp strands
and the bushes and hedges
had pointy ice hands.

The leafy trees glimmered
a dazzling crystal white
and the roofs were dusted
with powder overnight.

The icy mud puddles
went "crunch" beneath my feet.
I stomped out a rhythm-
a frozen cadence beat.

I puffed my billowy breath,
pretending to smoke.
I was off to work
and I was one happy bloke.

It was October
and I sure didn't miss June.
I puckered my lips
and whistled a happy tune.

I got to my truck
and saw something that I hate.
My windows were frosty.
I knew that I'd be late.

I snapped out of it
and hoped my job wasn't lost.
I grumbled upset and scraped off...
autumn's first frost!

October 12, 2013

Night Hazards

You switch off the hall light
and head towards your bedroom.
It's just a short walk
but now it's dark as a tomb.

You cross the bedroom
and smash your knee on the post.
You bellow, yelp and moan
like you're a wounded ghost.

Your child hollers out
for a drink of water.
You step on a Lego-
insert swearing blotter

Putting out the cat
you trip over someone's shoes.
You promise to that person
they'll too get a bruise.

Now the dog wants out.
You go to open the door
and slip in wet vomit
that's all over the floor.

Off to the bathroom
you're muttering all the way
when you bang right into
an ill placed TV tray.

You clean off your foot-
then go to wipe up the yack.
You catch your toe on the couch
with a solid crack.

You give up on it
and limp blindly back to bed.
Your leg is throbbing
and you feel halfway dead.

To avoid these dangerous
hazards of the night,
install in each of your rooms...
at least one night light!

October 19, 2013

Patchwork

A patchwork quilt tells a story
that's handed down through years.
Generations use them
'cause Gram made them for "little dears".

She sewed a baby's first charm quilt
for me when I was born.
I have it after all these years
though it's threadbare and torn.

When I turned five years old
she made me a "Sunbonnet Sue".
It covers my guest bedroom's bed
'cause I still have it too.

On my sweet sixteenth birthday
she gave me a friendship quilt.
It was made of fabric blocks
my aunties, mom and gram built.

I received an album quilt
when I married my true love.
It told my life's story
that Gram still follows from above.

I love all of these quilts
that my grandmother made for me.
More than that she taught me
the love of quilting at "the bee".

I made a memory quilt
to remind me of her life.
She was a devoted mother,
sister, grandma and wife.

Now I am the grandma
who wields the quilting bobbin.
This month it's up to me
to lead us all at "round robin."

So all of you ladies
loosen those sewing box latches
gather needle, thread and around...
let's all sew some patches!

October 26, 2013

The Witch

There's a spooky old house
that sits on Knob Hill.
Even in the daylight
it gives you a chill.

It's surrounded by
a rusty iron fence
guarded by a three-legged dog
named Suspense.

The flower beds are full
of deadly nightshade.
Hemlock and thistle
grow in a poison glade.

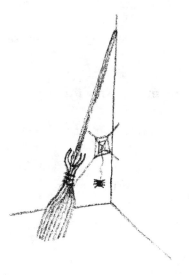

Black cats silhouette
the broken window frames.
Their eyes glow through cobwebs
sharp, bright yellow flames.

But scarier than the dog
or the plant itch-
scarier than the cats-
was the wicked witch!

She had long, stringy black hair
and yellow skin,
was wrinkled and hunched
with a snaggle-tooth grin.

We boys would peer
through the rusty iron bars.
The hag would appear-
we'd bolt like shooting stars.

"Come visit Granny
my small, sweet little dears!"
As we ran
her cackle would ring in our ears.

This Halloween we went there
trick-or-treating.
I passed the iron gate-
my heart stopped beating!

There was the witch
handing out treats from a pot!
"Come close little dears
and see what Granny's got!"

I reached inside the pot-
her hand grabbed my wrist!
"Come inside boy!"
I squirmed away with a twist.

I ran down the steps
and tripped over Suspense!
We both yelped! I jumped up
and ran for the fence.

Suddenly to my right
her dark figure loomed!
I ran through the yard,
tripped and fell. I was doomed!

I banged my knee hard
and fainted like a stone.
I awoke in a room
but wasn't alone.

A beautiful woman
was bathing my face.
I was in a fancy room
"Where is this place?"

"You banged your knee hard.
Does anything else hurt?"
I stared hard at her
then recognized her skirt!

"It's you! You're the witch!
You'll boil me in stew!"
"Hush now, dear little boy,
none of that is true!"

"I'm not really a witch.
It's all just pretend.
Before I send you home
I want you to mend."

She showed me her wig
and the mask that she wore
and how she made Suspense
have three legs- not four.

The thistles were plastic
and you can sure bet
the cats- adopted,
the house- a movie set.

I swore secrecy
before I went my way.
She filled my candy sack
and had this to say:

"It's my outer mask
that must always be seen
'cause my favorite holiday...
is Halloween!"

November 2, 2013

Autumn's Acoustics

Each autumn brings
special music to the air
presented by the leaves
with symphonic flair!

flip-flap-flutter-flap
They quiver in the trees.

whoop-whap-whipper-whap
They break loose in the breeze.

swish-swoosh-swisher-swoosh
Cars spin them as they pass.

rar-roar-rever-roar
The blower clears the grass.

shake-shook-shaker-shook
They're raked into piles.

splish-splash-sploosher-splash
Kids jump in with smiles.

stuff-sluff-stuffer-sluff
They're shoved tight into sacks.

snip-snap-snipper-snap
They burn with pops and cracks.

But their most melodious
and rhythmic beat
occurs when they're crunch, crunching...
beneath my feet!

Sunday, November 3, 2013 TPNH Special Edition

This poem appeared in the "Life in the Bitterroot" section. It tells the story of the visitor's information cabin that sits atop Lost Trail Pass. Bert, a Bitterroot Valley Chamber of Commerce volunteer, compiled her summer experiences as a visitor's guide and gave them to me as a resource to write this poem.

The Cabin

At the height of
seven thousand and fourteen feet,
I'm at Lost Trail Pass
where visitors I greet.

I'm a log cabin
set on the side of the road,
where weary travelers can rest
and set down their load.

I'm chock full of brochures
of places not to miss.
You get them with explanations
from Bert or Chris.

When you stop to chat to them
know they are alone.
You see, there's no computer
or even cell phone!

There are deer, squirrels, birds-
an occasional bear-
and the cutest darn chipmunks
running everywhere!

This summer was great
for passing information
to eager travelers
enjoying vacation.

About one hundred people
stopped in every day,
all with great stories
as they travel on their way.

Most come in their pickup
or a passenger car,
from every corner of the map
both near and far.

Japan, Mexico, Vermont,
Europe, Idaho,
Canada, Switzerland...
the list goes on you know!

Most folks are from the states
driving around the west,
and hundreds of bicyclists.
I do not jest!

Pedaling across the state
or the country you know,
it's amazing how their legs
keep them on the go!

Other two-wheelers
are motorcycles galore!
They stop in and visit,
then head off with a roar.

Small tent campers, huge RV's
and travel trailers,
homes of the nomadic
countryside land sailors.

Let's not forget determined
hikers and walkers,
trekking cross country-
all of them eager talkers!

The weather on the pass
varies from day to day,
sometimes wet and cold
but it never stays that way.

The sun always comes out
to greet the friendly folk,
late this summer
he was behind all of the smoke.

My pet area was hard
for people to find.
Either I need a bigger sign
or they're all blind!

Maps and good info
were passed out all summer long,
but I did have something
that went dreadfully wrong.

Late one night vandals struck
and turned me upside down!
They broke out a window
and really went to town.

They broke my cabinets, signs,
and my huge wall showcase.
They threw my pamphlets and plants
all over the place.

It took days to clean
from these unwanted callers.
They made off with a total
of eight whole dollars!

Other than that incident,
my summer was fun,
and I'm looking ahead
to the next fun-filled one!

I hope to see you folks
up on the pass next year.
You're all welcome.
I want that to be crystal clear.

But don't wait for your own
invite in the mail.
Take a scenic drive for info...
to Lost Trail!

Out For Pie

After the play Friday night
we went out for pie.
Being late, I guessed
it would be my wife and I.

I thought a couple of truckers
might be in there.
As we sat down
I couldn't help but gawk and stare.

There was the town cat lady
in the corner booth
with an unlit cigarette
in her missing tooth.

Sitting at a table
there were six college kids
spilling cream everywhere
by popping off the lids.

At the counter there was
a shabbily dressed bum
muttering to his coffee,
"I wish you were rum."

Some blue haired ladies
clucked around a Scrabble board
squabbling about how the word
"jinx" should be scored.

At a table by himself
was a blocked writer
yanking on his hair
and pulling an all-nighter.

Taking up three booths
was a large group of "goth" teens
in a role playing tourney
making quite a scene.

Our bleary eyed waitress
looked like a freight train wreck.
I said this to my wife
as I picked up the check,

"For first class entertainment
there's nothing finer
than watching customers...
in an all night diner!"

November 9, 2013

Taking Care

To protect me from a cold
I wear an amber bead.
I want to grow very old
so I chewed a grape seed.

I only sleep in a bed
that's laying north to south
if there's a hat on my head-
I don't want a dry mouth.

If a black cat crosses me,
I quickly cross his path.
It's the only way, you see
to not drown in the bath.

I never walk underneath
a ladder opened wide.
I don't want a funeral wreath
propped up along my side.

I really love my mother
so I don't step on cracks.
As for my toast- I smother
both the fronts and the backs.

A broken mirror's bad luck
that will last seven years
and since I'm really no schmuck,
I avoid them my dears.

I eat a Red Delicious
to keep the doc away.
Don't call me superstitious...
I'm just heedful, I say!

November 16, 2013

Bridge Club

It was Saturday morning
at the bridge club.
A table of four
were making quite a hub.

These four silver tops
were talking about men.
"It's your bid, Ruth. By the way,
how is your Ken?"

"Oh, Jean! You know he's not mine!
He's far too fat.
He just takes me to the buffet-
and that's that."

"I want a thinner man
with gas in his tank.
I pass. Now Jean,
tell us all about your Hank."

"Oh that Hank!
He's got a heart of solid gold.
I bid one spade. And Hank-
well, he's far too old."

"I want a younger man
who's vibrant and strong.
It's your bid, Lily.
What's taking you so long?"

"I'm gonna pass.
Have I told you about Joe?
He's still quite young
but his girlfriend's gotta go."

"Why Lily! You and Joe
are sneaking around!?"
"Oh, yes. It's quite fun
trying not to be found!"

"Bea, lay your dummy hand down
so we can play.
And how about you?
What do you have to say?"

"I can tell you this girls
the man that I crave
is rich, single...
and has one foot in the grave!"

November 23, 2013

Her Apron

I awoke early.
'Twas an hour before dawn.
I stepped in the kitchen-
and slipped her apron on.

It always hangs on the back
of the pantry door.
I wear it on special days-
not for routine chore.

A week ago I wore it
to make the fresh dough
I'd use for dinner rolls-
and bread stuffing you know.

That same day I baked
a fresh batch of pumpkin pies.
Also apple, and her favorite-
mincemeat surprise!

Monday night I wore it too
for orange date nut bread.
We have it Friday morning-
with a cream cheese spread.

Making her secret eggnog,
I wore it last night
and thawed the turkey in the sink-
the fit was tight.

This morning I took the stuffing
and filled that bird.
Then followed her Jell-O recipe-
word for word.

I started the potatoes,
both the mashed and sweet,
with the marshmallows on top-
always such a treat.

With the relish tray done
I was ready for guests.
She referred to them as-
"her necessary pests".

I poured some wine
and glanced at her cranberry dish.
I raised my glass to her-
and made a secret wish.

Though she won't be here for dinner,
this you can see,
when I wear her apron...
my mom's right here with me.

November 30, 2013

Friday

After filling up on all
that we're thankful for
we form a riot
at the entrance of the store.

A few hours ago
we ate with those we love.
Now we jostle for a spot
with a friendly shove.

We cherished our time spent
with those we hold so dear,
but those times are done-
door buster deals are here!

It's three in the morning
and we're all feeling rushed.
The manager opens up
and gets himself crushed!

It's a race to the toasters.
They're three ninety eight!
I got kicked in the ribs-
some guy just couldn't wait.

I sprinted on over
to the DVD case!
I reached for a movie
and got punched in the face.

I went for a flat screen!
But I got my hair pulled.
I ended up on hands and knees
in a choke hold.

I lunged for a new laptop!
I got my eye jabbed.
I got off easy-
the guy next to me was stabbed.

After fifteen hours
of holiday spirit
I got back to my car
but could barely steer it.

There should be a change
and if I had it my way
from now on it would be called...
"black and blue Friday!"

December 7, 2013

Firewood

Now winter's icy grip
is finally here,
I think back to childhood-
thoughts not so dear.

I spent all of my summers
on firewood,
although I dodged it
anytime that I could.

First we'd cut it
chainsaw noise, gas and sawdust.
The saw wouldn't run
no matter how you cussed.

Next you'd split it up
by hand with an old axe.
Then haul it to the shed
and put it in neat stacks.

There was sticky sap
and splinters in your arms
and those gross stink bugs-
lacking all sorts of charms.

Winter would come
and I'd have to haul it in
and chop it small
to fill the kindling bin.

We'd wake in the morning
to a frigid home.
Try lighting the fire-
your mouth starts to foam.

If your house isn't freezing,
it's blazing hot.
To dump the ashes-
you need to find a spot.

Now that I'm grown
I choose to heat without wood.
There's a lawn hammock
where the woodshed once stood.

No matter how low
the outside temp is at
I walk over...
and adjust my thermostat!

December 14, 2013

Silver Bells

"It's Christmas time in the city"
so the song goes.
For me the indications
come right through my nose.

In through my front door
past the round evergreen wreath,
it's scent mingles with the fir
with presents beneath.

I hang my coat near
the woodstove's chimney pipe
and smell the lodge pole smoke.
It's my favorite type.

There's a bowl of fresh popcorn
popped to string the tree
I take a whiff-
and gobble a kernel or three.

I step in the kitchen.
There's cider on the stove.
It's essence tickles my nose-
cinnamon and clove.

My wife's coffee
has eggnog in it- with nutmeg.
Before I take a sip
I breathe in a deep drag.

Her kitchen is a bouquet
of baking perfume.
The scent of jam-jams
and pepper-nuts fill the room.

They say it's Christmas time
when you hear "Silver Bells"
but I know when it's time...
by the way my house smells!

December 21, 2013

The magic and mystery of Santa Claus is a part of childhood that many storytellers touch on. Here is my attempt:

Crumbs

It was Christmas Eve
and I couldn't sleep a wink.
I was just lying there
when I heard a strange "clink".

I slid out of bed
and crept slowly down the hall,
peeked 'round the corner,
saw our stockings on the wall.

They were filled to the brim
with fruit, trinkets and toys!
I had been a good girl
and my brothers- good boys.

By the lights on the tree
I saw more toys and games.
I knew some were mine.
I just couldn't see the names.

I heard the "clink" again
and sneaked into the room.
I saw a large man in red
working in the gloom.

I froze in my tracks
and was quiet as a mouse.
It was Santa Claus-
building me a new dollhouse!

I glanced at the stand
where the milk and cookies were.
They were eaten up-
it was Santa Claus for sure!

"Hi Santa" I whispered.
He 'bout jumped through the roof.
He turned and smiled,
"Back to bed, you little goof!"

It was Daddy in red PJ's
up working late.
"I have to help Santa," he said.
"His load can't wait."

He scooped me up
and carried me back to my bed.
Lots and lots of questions
raced through my little head.

"Why was Daddy working?"
"Didn't Santa have elves?"
"How about the cookies?
They couldn't eat themselves."

As Daddy kissed my cheek
and tucked me tight back in,
I lay there puzzling...
'bout the crumbs on his chin.

December 28, 2013

Work Ethic

As I say, "Goodbye"
to another long work year,
I'll charge into the new
in my uppermost gear.

I'll be first at work
by half an hour or more
and when the "whistle blows"
I'll be last out the door.

With blinding speed
I'll respond to each e-mail
and promptly return calls
each day without fail.

Within the first week
my desk will be clutter free.
The base of my in-box
will be easy to see.

My organizing skills
will be second to none.
As for productivity-
I'll be number one.

And with the big boss,
I'll be his top, go-to guy.
My coworkers will be green-
wait a minute! Why!?

I might be at my job
getting lots of work done
as a stick in the mud
having no friends or fun.

So I'll skate on by
and get cured of this fever
because nobody likes...
an over-achiever!

January 3, 2014

The Squinter

I'm not the best driver
as most of you know
but I'm at my worst
in winter's ice and snow.

In the city on the ice
I drive too fast
and slide all around
like a puck being passed.

At intersections
I forget to pump brakes.
To even stop me
road gravel's what it takes.

For me corners are bad
but hills are the worst.
I barely make it down
even when in first.

And driving on the highway
if I change lanes,
I 'bout go in the ditch
unless I have chains.

My hardest part of driving
in the winter
is when I have to be
a morning squinter.

I peer out straight ahead
with tight eye squinches
'cause my defroster's thawed...
just a few inches!

January 11, 2014

I always have plenty of ideas for poems. Readers will often ask if I ever get writer's block. I don't, but I can imagine what it would be like, so I wrote a poem about it.

The Writer

I've run out of ideas
and my poem is due.
I rack my brain
but I just don't have a clue.

Up and down, back and forth
I pace the night floor.
Needing some fresh air
I step out the back door.

I stare up at the night sky
and ask the stars.
They don't answer.
Neither do the moon or Mars.

I go back inside.
Maybe I need a snack.
I ask my pretzel sticks.
They don't answer back.

I throw myself back down
in my easy chair.
I clench my teeth, wring my fists
and yank my hair.

I brew some fresh coffee
and fill my mug up.
I plead with it
but nothing comes from the cup.

I stare at my paper
and motionless pen.
With fists I pound my head
again and again.

I'm startled by the chiming
of the wall clock
saying, "It's two a.m."
It's willing to talk.

Looks like I'll pull
another long all-nighter.
That's the trouble with being...
a blocked writer!

January 18, 2014

The White Stuff

This Saturday morning
I popped out of bed.
"There's no school," I thought.
"I can't wait to sled!"

I ate a bowl
of piping hot oatmeal.
"Breakfast before playing."
That was Mom's deal.

I pulled on my snow pants
and zipped up my coat,
laced up my boots
and wrapped a scarf 'round my throat.

I yanked on gloves,
put a hat on my noggin,
went to the garage
and grabbed my toboggan.

My breath billowed
as I stepped out in the chill.
I trudged through the back field
and up the hill.

When I got to the top
I looked all around
and felt discouraged
about the barren ground.

It was freezing cold
but there was no white stuff.
I shouted up at the sky-
I'd had enough.

"Old Man Winter
there's one thing I want to know.
It's mid-January...
now where's all the snow!?"

January 25, 2014

Move It

"Dear, I can't seem to find
my keys anywhere."
"Well pick up the newspaper.
See, they're right there!"

"I thought you said
my chili was on this shelf."
"Move these peaches.
You could have done it yourself!"

"Hon, don't you keep the scissors
in the top drawer?"
"Lift the envelopes.
It's not such a hard chore!"

"Darling, aren't there socks
in this basket of clothes?"
"Under the towels.
Did you think to lift those!?"

"I had a book
but it's nowhere to be seen."
"Except right here-
beneath your own magazine!"

"My wool hat is lost.
This really gets my goat."
"Well Billy Scruff,
did you look under your coat!?"

Conversations like these
happen every day
and to summarize it
I'd just like to say:

When a man's looking
but can't seem to find it,
a woman moves one thing...
it's right behind it!

February 1, 2014

The Big Game

My wife and I sat down
for Sunday's football game.
I hoped she would enjoy it
and not think it lame.

I would explain the rules
and describe the teams
emphasizing a win
would complete all their dreams.

I prepared some healthy snacks
I knew she would like.
She criticized the anthem
belted through the mike.

After kickoff she said
who she was rooting for.
I found out it was based on
the colors they wore.

As the game went on
she didn't seem to be bored.
She hollered really loud
each time either team scored.

I explained that most men
don't watch the halftime show.
She pointed out I should find
some place else to go.

The game resumed and became
a long drawn out fight
but she hung in there
and watched late into the night.

When the game was over
and the trophy lifted
I tried to recap
but her attention drifted.

I talked clock management
and the onside kick try
and how the ref's calls
could have helped the other guy.

She became more distant
the longer that I talked.
Frankly, she told the truth.
I couldn't be more shocked.

"The interference calls
were both 'controversials'."
"I'm sorry dear, I just watched...
for the commercials!"

February 8, 2014

Cold Snap

I was awoken this morning
by the cold.
"Sub-zero temperatures"
is what I was told.

I'd go to the back door
to see for myself.
I put on my slippers
and specs from the shelf.

As I neared the door
there was frost on the pane
and ice had formed
on my security chain.

I could feel the chill
coming through the door
especially by my feet
down on the floor.

I peered out the window
at the morning sky.
It was cloudless
with ice crystals floating by.

The cat's water dish
was a solid ice block.
He was on the bed spread
sleeping like a rock.

These signs pointed
to sub-zero temperature.
I'd check the thermometer
just to be sure.

Then a bigger indicator
than all those.
I took a step outside...
and my boogers froze!

February 15, 2014

All's Fair...

One snowy day
a few boys got together
to build a fort
in February's weather.

The snow packed firm.
Of the walls the boys were proud.
Then they placed a sign that read:
"No girls allowed".

Well it just so happened
on that very day
a few young girls
were in the field to play.

The girls crossed the field
to talk to the boys.
The boys jeered at them
and made lots of rude noise.

"Hey boys, guess what this fort
would be perfect for?
Let's use it to play house!"
"No! This fort's for war!"

With wild whooping
the boys snatched up some snow
then they charged at the girls
and started to throw.

Across the field-
running fast the girls fled
to a stash of snowballs
hidden in a sled!

The tide quickly turned
the boys knew they were squashed.
They were overpowered,
pummeled and white-washed.

"Retreat, men! Retreat!
It's our only resort!
These girls are too strong.
Head back to the snow fort!"

The girls raced them back.
They won and staked their claim.
"This is our club now
and "House" is the new game.

You boys can stay
without any dues or fines.
You just have to swear...
to be our Valentine's!

February 22, 2014

The Truth

"Hey Ellie! Where are you?
I'm calling your name!
Come on- answer me!
I'm not playing this game!"

"I'm right here, Mom."
"Where the world have you been?"
"Would you believe
I was feeding a blue hen?"

"She had babies
the colors of the rainbow.
I fed her green worms
that in the dark would glow."

"Then I tracked an outlaw
named Slapjack Celeste.
She ate rattlesnakes
and terrorized the west."

"I scampered in walls
with a family of mice.
We robbed the pantry
of cookies, bread and rice."

"After that snack
I boarded a rocket ship.
Was nabbed by space creatures,
but gave them the slip."

"I joined a side show
after growing a beard.
It grew one foot per day
which was really weird."

"I met a mean princess.
Her name was Alice.
The king had to build her
a golden palace."

"Ellie, what have I
told you about lying?
You're doing it now
without even trying!"

"Mom, I'm sure not trying
to be misleading.
It's just my way of saying...
I was reading!"

The Rings

Every four years we gather
in the ice and snow
to see how high, how fast
and how far we can go.

On skis, skates and snowboards
we endure long races.
We end with tears of joy
or defeat on our faces.

Soaring through the air,
spinning phenomenal flips,
perfection brings a winning smile
to your lips.

Balancing on a single
metal skating blade,
if you land all your jumps
you just might have it made.

Shoot your target, curl your stone,
score in the net,
skate around the long track
with your fastest time yet.

Skeleton, luge and bobsled
on an icy track.
You push of with full force
and don't even look back.

Either speed on the track
or distance through the air
done beneath the flame
with its unwavering flare.

Human spirit takes flight
and soars on widespread wings
when the world unites...
beneath Olympic rings.

March 1, 2014

The Shoveler

For the last two days
it's done nothing but snow.
I've been amused
watching out my window.

The flakes mesmerize me
as they gently fall.
What I'm really watching
is my neighbor, Paul.

He's a short thin man
with overly large feet.
Wearing a red wool hat,
he scurries the street.

He clears his driveway
with a frantic zip-zip.
I smile a bit
and drink my coffee- sip, sip.

He finished his drive,
then started on the walks
as fast as a sprinter
off the starting blocks.

I get the willies
from the gravel's crunch, crunch.
To cover the noise
I eat cookies- munch, munch.

He spreads out some salt
and thinks he's all done now.
Before he can blink-
here comes the city plow!

His shouting's muffled
by the plow engine's roar.
My laughing is muffled
by my kitchen door.

Paul begins clearing
outside of his hovel.
I step out and yell
at the human shovel.

"Sick of shoveling
what Old Man Winter dealt?
You should do what I do...
wait for it to melt!"

BONUS POEMS

Pitch Black

You're taking out the trash.
It's pitch black outside.
You're not sure
where the wild animals hide.

You forgot something important
in your car.
You're sure a thug will get you
though it's not far.

You have to get the mail.
You need a bill.
But there's a murderer
looking for a kill.

You have to go out
and find your kitty-cat.
You hear a twig snap behind you–
"What was that!?"

You rush back in
fast as an electric spark!
You could win gold…
if the race was in the dark!

Metrical Composition

Balladry on the sea?
That's poetry in ocean.

Doggerel on hand cream?
That's poetry with lotion.

Rhyming on wizardry?
That's poetry with potion.

Verse on a wild whim?
That's poetry with notion.

Rune with Austrian coins?
That's poetry on groschen.

These stanzas on a bus?
That's poetry in motion.

Rime with extra duties?
That's poetry promotion.

Poesy stripped of its rank?
That's poetry demotion.

Paean sung joyfully?
That's poetry devotion.

Rhyme with copious tears?
That's poetry emotion.

Versification slack?
That's poetry slow motion.

All the poems on this list?
It's poetry commotion!

Wishes

If wishes were horses,
beggars would ride.

If wishes were blue kites,
children would glide.

If wishes were play grounds,
children would slide.

If wishes were seek games,
children would hide.

If wishes were oceans,
they'd splash the tide.

If wishes were sunshine,
they'd be outside.

But wishes aren't horses,
playgrounds or blue kites,
nor oceans or sunshine,
or seek games at night.

Wishes are inside you,
where no one else can see,
and wishes will make you,
whatever you want to be.

So wish with your whole heart,
and wish with your whole mind,
believe in your wishes...
they'll come true, you will find!

Fingers Crossed

Cross your fingers
if you want good luck
and hope you don't
get hit by a truck.

Cross your heart
when you make a vow.
You'll keep your word
from then 'til now.

Cross your eyes
and you will see double.
To walk straight
you will have some trouble.

Cross your legs
when you really gotta go,
and wave your hand
so your teacher will know!

The Happy Hippie

This is the ballad
of the happy hippie
who now leads a new life
that's not so trippy.

He's traded in his
canvas shoes and hemp socks
for his weekend pair of
comfy Birkenstocks.

His V.W. bus
is long put away.
He drives a Subaru now,
day after day.

And that really bright colored
spotted tie dye?
He's traded those threads in
for a suit and tie.

As for the round, wire
John Lennon glasses,
he's got clear contacts now
and joined the masses.

His mane was once
a long, straight pony tail,
but his hair's trimmed monthly now
without fail.

He never was without
his colorful beads.
Now it's his PDA
and cell phone he needs.

All the Beatles music
he does still applaud,
but no longer vinyl–
it's on his iPod.

It's ballroom and jazz now,
not the disco dance
and Armani khakis,
not bell-bottom pants.

And the handkerchief headband
is long, long gone.
Now a visor
when he gets his golf game on.

Times have certainly changed
and with that he's fine.
He still says "goodbye"...
by flashing the peace sign.